THE INDIAN ROYALTY

A CULTURAL AND HISTORICAL EXPLORATION OF INDIA'S MAHARAJAS AND THEIR KINGDOM

DR. JAGADEESH PILLAI

Made with ♥ on the Notion Press Platform
www.notionpress.com

|| Dedicated to all wisdom seekers around the World ||

ॐ

Contents

Contents

Prayer

**"Om Bhadram Karnebhih Shrunuyaama
DevaahBhadram Pashyemaakshabhiryajatraah
Sthirairangaistushtuvaamsastanoobhih Vyashema
Devahitam YadaayuhSwasti Na Indro
VridhashravaahSwasti Nah Pooshaa
VishwavedaahSwasti Nastaarkshyo ArishtanemihSwasti
No Brihaspatir DadhaatuOm Shantih, Shantih, Shantih"**

The literal meaning of this mantra is: OM. O Gods! Let us hear auspicious words from our ears. O reverent Gods! Let us behold propitious visions from our eyes, let our organs and body be stable, healthy, and strong. Let us do that which is pleasing to the gods in the life span allotted to us. May Indra, inscribed in the scriptures, bring us fortune! May Pushan, the knower of the world, grant us prosperity! May Trakshya, who vanquishes enemies, bestow us with blessings! May Brihaspati bring us success!
OM Peace, Peace, Peace.

About The Author

Dr. Jagadeesh Pillai is a renowned Guinness World Record holder, writer, and researcher hailing from Varanasi, also known as the abode of Lord Shiva. With a Ph.D. in Vedic Science and a range of creative ideas and achievements, he is a true polymath. He is the author of more than 100 books including Research Publications. Although his roots can be traced back to Kerala, the people of Varanasi hold him in high regard and affectionately consider him one of their own.

In 1998, Dr. Pillai was offered a job at Banaras Hindu University, but he left the position after only two months to pursue greater goals in life. He believed that in order to study Indian scriptures and engage in other creative endeavours, he needed to retire from the daily grind of working solely for money at a young age.

He started an export business from scratch, using the knowledge he had gained from a previous job in the industry. His intelligence and unique approach to business led to great success in a short period of time, earning him more in just a decade and a half than he would have in a lifetime working in a government job. Upon the passing of Dr. APJ Abdul Kalam, Dr. Pillai decided to leave the business and dedicate himself to reading, studying, researching, and experimenting.

During his tenure in the export business, Dr. Pillai traveled to over 16 countries, gaining valuable insight and experiencing the world and life in detail.

Dr. Pillai has achieved four Guinness World Records in the following subjects:

"Script to Screen" - In this record, Dr. Pillai produced and directed an animation film within the shortest time possible, breaking the previous record set by Canadians. He has also received numerous national and international awards and recognitions for this achievement.

Longest Line of Postcards - For this record, Dr. Pillai created a line of 16,300 postcards on the occasion of the 163rd anniversary of Indian Postal Day. The event also included a questionnaire about the Indian flag.

Largest Poster Awareness Campaign - Dr. Pillai designed an awareness campaign on the subject of "Beti Bachao - Beti Padhao" (Save the Girl Child - Educate the Girl Child) to achieve this record.

Largest Envelope - In tribute to the Indian Prime Minister's "Make in India" initiative, Dr. Pillai created a 4000 square meter envelope using waste paper to achieve this record.

Attempted - **70000 Candles on a 210 kg Cake** - To celebrate the 70th Indian Independence Day, Dr. Pillai attempted to light 70,000 candles on a 210 kg cake, which was recorded in World Records India.

Attempted - **Documentary on Dhamek Stupa of Sarnath in 17 Languages** - Dr. Pillai attempted to create a documentary on the Dhamek Stupa of Sarnath, dubbing it in 17 different languages. The result of this attempt is currently awaiting confirmation from the Guinness World Records.

Dr. Pillai is skilled in teaching the Bhagavad Gita, a Hindu scripture, and is popular among young people. He has helped many young people improve their lives through his motivational teachings.

In addition to teaching, he has composed and sung numerous Sanskrit Bhajans and patriotic songs.

He has also written and directed several short films and documentaries for awareness campaigns, and has volunteered with the police in both UP and Kerala to spread awareness about various issues through videos and photography.

Incredibly, he has produced and directed over 100 documentaries about the city of Varanasi, all on his own.

He has also helped and guided more than 25 boys and girls to achieve world records through creative and innovative methods. He is a multifaceted person who uses his intellect and the blessings given to him by God to excel in various areas. He is both a teacher and a student, always learning and teaching, and is able to master any subject he comes across.

He is a selfless social activist and motivational speaker who has overcome struggles and failures to become a successful and enthusiastic individual with a rich life experience.

In addition to his work with the Bhagavad Gita, he is also an efficient Tarot card reader, Astro-Vastu consultant, and a talented singer and composer. He has sung the entire Ram Charita Manas and Bhagavad Gita in his own compositions, and has sung the phrase "Lokah Samastha Sukhino Bhavantu" in 50 different languages. He is currently working on a detailed and scientific study of Vedas, Upanishads, Puranas, and the Bhagavad Gita. He has also composed and sung the Hanuman Chalisa and Gayatri Mantra in 108 and 1008 different compositions, respectively.

Awards - Four Times Guinness World Records, Winner of Mahatma Gandhi Vishwa Shanti Puraskar, Mahatma Gandhi Global Peace Ambassador, Kashi Ratna Award, Dr. APJ Abdul Kalam Motivational Person of the Year 2017, Mother Teresa Award, Indira Gandhi Priyadarshini Award, Bharat Vikas Ratna Award, Udyog Ratna Award, Vigyan Prasar Award, Poorvanchal Ratn Samman.

Preface

The Indian Royalty: A Cultural and Historical Exploration of India's Maharajas and their Kingdoms is an exciting new book that delves into the fascinating history of India's royal families. From the Mughal Empire to the present day, this book provides an in-depth look at the culture, customs, and traditions of India's Maharajas and their kingdoms.

This book is a comprehensive exploration of the history and culture of India's royal families. It covers the rise and fall of the Mughal Empire, the emergence of the British Raj, and the modern-day Maharajas. It also examines the customs and traditions of the royal families, their lifestyles, and their impact on India's culture and history.

The Indian Royalty is an invaluable resource for anyone interested in learning more about India's royal families. It provides an insightful look into the culture and history of India's Maharajas and their kingdoms. It is an essential read for anyone interested in understanding the history and culture of India's royal families.

This book is an engaging and informative read that will captivate readers of all ages. It is an essential resource for anyone interested in learning more about India's royal families and their impact on India's culture and history. With its comprehensive coverage of the culture, customs, and traditions of India's Maharajas and their kingdoms, The Indian Royalty is a must-read for anyone interested in understanding the history and culture of India's royal families.

I

Introduction: Understanding Indian Royalty

The Indian Royalty has long been a source of fascination for many. From the grandeur of their palaces to the intricate details of their customs, the Maharajas of India have captivated the imaginations of people around the world. This book, The Indian Royalty: A Cultural and Historical Exploration of India's Maharajas and their Kingdoms, seeks to explore the history and culture of these powerful rulers.

The Maharajas of India were the rulers of princely states, which were semi-autonomous regions that were part of the British Raj. These rulers were powerful and influential, and their kingdoms were often vast and wealthy. They were also deeply rooted in tradition and culture, and their customs and practices were often unique and fascinating.

The Maharajas of India were also known for their lavish lifestyles. They lived in grand palaces, surrounded by luxurious gardens and courtyards. They were often accompanied by a large entourage of servants and attendants, and they were known for their extravagant feasts and parties.

The Maharajas of India were also known for their patronage of the arts. They were patrons of music, dance, and literature, and they often commissioned works of art and architecture. They were also patrons of education, and many of them established schools and universities.

The Maharajas of India were also known for their political power. They were often involved in the politics of their kingdoms, and they were often consulted by the British Raj on matters of state. They were also known for their diplomatic skills, and they often acted as mediators between the British Raj and other princely states.

The Maharajas of India were also known for their philanthropy. They often donated large sums of money to charities and causes, and they were often involved in the welfare of their people.

The Maharajas of India were known for their wealth, power, and grandeur. However, beyond their regal status, they were also known for their philanthropy and their commitment to the welfare of their people. These rulers, who hailed from various princely states across India, left an indelible impact on the cultural and historical landscape of the country.

One of the most notable examples of the philanthropy of the Indian Maharajas was the Jamsaheb of Nawanagar, also known as Jam Sahib of Jamnagar, who made substantial contributions to various causes such as education, healthcare, and the environment. He founded the Shri Bhadranaya Seva Trust, which provided medical care to the poor, and he also established schools, colleges, and research institutes.

Another example of the philanthropic efforts of the Maharajas was the donation of the Gaekwad family of Baroda. The Gaekwads, who ruled over the state of Baroda, donated large sums of money to various charitable causes, including the construction of hospitals, schools, and orphanages. They were also instrumental in supporting the arts, and they were known for their love of music, dance, and literature.

The Maharajas were also known for their support of the welfare of their people. For instance, the Maharaja of Mysore, who ruled over the state of Mysore, was renowned for his progressive policies and initiatives aimed at improving the lives of his people. He built schools and hospitals, and he also implemented various reforms aimed at improving the lives of the poor and the marginalized.

Despite the abolition of the princely states in India in the mid-twentieth century, the legacy of the Indian Maharajas continues to influence the cultural and historical landscape of the country. Many of the institutions and causes that they supported continue to thrive, and their contributions have been remembered and celebrated by generations of Indians.

The Indian Maharajas left a lasting impact on the country through their philanthropy and commitment to the welfare of their people. Their legacy serves as a reminder of the important role that cultural and historical figures can play in shaping the future of a nation, and it continues to inspire future generations to contribute to the greater good.

India's royal families have left an indelible mark on the country's culture and history.

ꕥ

II

The Maharajas of the Rajputs: Rajasthan

The Maharajas of the Rajputs: Rajasthan have a long and storied history, stretching back centuries. These powerful rulers were the most influential and powerful of all the Rajputs, and their legacy is still felt today. The Rajputs were a warrior caste, and their kingdom was one of the most powerful in India. They were known for their bravery and loyalty, and their kingdom was renowned for its wealth and grandeur.

The Maharajas of the Rajputs: Rajasthan were renowned for their lavish lifestyles and their patronage of the arts. They were patrons of literature, music, and the visual arts, and their courts were renowned for their grandeur and opulence. The Maharajas were also known for their patronage of education, and many of the great universities of India were founded during their reign.

The Maharajas of the Rajputs: Rajasthan were also known for their military prowess. They were renowned for their skill in battle, and their armies were feared throughout India. They were also known for their diplomatic skills, and their kingdom was often sought after by other rulers for alliances and treaties.

The Maharajas of the Rajputs: Rajasthan were also known for their religious tolerance. They were tolerant of all religions, and their kingdom was a haven for religious minorities. They were also known for their patronage of the arts, and their courts were renowned for their grandeur and opulence.

The legacy of the Maharajas of the Rajputs: Rajasthan is still felt today. Their kingdom was one of the most powerful in India, and their influence is still seen in the culture and architecture of the region. Their tolerance towards different religions has contributed to the rich cultural diversity of Rajasthan, which is still visible today in the form of various religious monuments and festivals. The Rajputs' patronage of the arts has resulted in the creation of magnificent palaces, temples, and havelis (traditional mansions), many of which have been preserved and are now popular tourist attractions. The grandeur and opulence of the Rajput courts are still remembered and celebrated, and have become an integral part of Rajasthan's cultural heritage.

From the intricate architecture of the forts and palaces to the intricate customs and traditions, the Indian royalty has been a source of fascination for centuries.

ꕥ

III

The Maharajas of the Marathas: Maharashtra

The Maharajas of the Marathas: Maharashtra have a long and storied history that is deeply intertwined with the culture and history of India. For centuries, the Marathas have been a powerful force in the region, and their influence can still be seen today.

The Marathas were a confederacy of Hindu warrior clans that rose to prominence in the 16th century. They were led by the great warrior king Shivaji, who established the Maratha Empire in 1674. Shivaji was a brilliant military strategist and a great leader, and his legacy is still celebrated today.

The Marathas were a powerful force in the region, and their influence extended far beyond the borders of Maharashtra. They were a major player in the politics of the Mughal

Empire, and they were also involved in the wars between the Mughals and the British.

The Marathas were also known for their patronage of the arts and culture. They were great patrons of literature, music, and the visual arts, and they were also known for their patronage of Hindu temples and shrines.

The Marathas were also known for their great military prowess. They were renowned for their cavalry and infantry, and they were also known for their use of guerrilla tactics. They were also known for their use of fortifications, and they were able to successfully defend their territories against the Mughals and the British.

The Marathas were also known for their great administrative skills. They were able to maintain a strong and efficient bureaucracy, and they were also able to maintain a strong and stable economy.

The Marathas were also known for their religious tolerance. They were tolerant of all religions, and they were also known for their respect for other cultures.

The Marathas were also known for their great achievements in the fields of science and technology. They were able to make great advances in the fields of mathematics, astronomy, and medicine, and their scholars made significant contributions to these fields. Additionally, the Maratha empire was known for its strong military, which was a significant factor in their rise to power and their ability to establish a vast empire that covered much of India.

The legacy of the Marathas is still felt today in India, where they are remembered for their religious tolerance, respect for other cultures, and scientific achievements. The Maratha dynasty has left a lasting impact on Indian history and culture, and their achievements continue to inspire future generations.

"The Indian royalty is a living testament to the grandeur and magnificence of India's past

ည

IV

The Maharajas of the Mughals: Delhi

The Mughal Empire was one of the most powerful and influential empires in India's history. The Mughal dynasty was founded in 1526 by Babur, a Central Asian ruler, and lasted until 1857 when the British Raj took control of India. The Mughal Empire was centered in Delhi and was ruled by a succession of powerful emperors, known as the Maharajas.

The Mughal Empire was renowned for its grandeur and opulence, and the Maharajas of Delhi were no exception. The Mughal rulers of Delhi were renowned for their lavish lifestyles, extravagant palaces, and grandiose monuments. The Mughal rulers of Delhi were also renowned for their patronage of the arts, and their patronage of literature, music, and architecture.

The Mughal rulers of Delhi were also renowned for their

religious tolerance. The Mughal rulers of Delhi were tolerant of all religions, and allowed people of all faiths to practice their religion freely. This religious tolerance was a major factor in the success of the Mughal Empire.

The Mughal rulers of Delhi were also renowned for their military prowess. The Mughal rulers of Delhi were able to expand their empire through military conquest, and were able to maintain their power through a strong military presence. The Mughal rulers of Delhi were also able to maintain their power through alliances with other powerful rulers in India.

The Mughal rulers of Delhi were also renowned for their patronage of the arts. The Mughal rulers of Delhi were patrons of literature, music, and architecture, and were responsible for the construction of many grand monuments and palaces. The Mughal rulers of Delhi were also responsible for the development of many of India's most famous monuments, such as the Taj Mahal and the Red Fort.

The Mughal rulers of Delhi were also renowned for their patronage of education. The Mughal rulers of Delhi were responsible for setting up numerous institutions of learning, such as madrasas, which were dedicated to the study of Islamic law, theology, and other subjects. During the Mughal era, the arts and sciences flourished, and many great works of literature, music, and architecture were produced. The Mughals also encouraged the exchange of ideas and cultural traditions between India and other parts of the world, leading to a rich fusion of cultures.

The legacy of the Mughal rulers of Delhi is still felt today in India, where their monuments and palaces continue to be popular tourist attractions and are considered architectural marvels. The Mughals' patronage of the arts and education has had a lasting impact on Indian culture, and their achievements continue to inspire future generations.

"It is a reminder of the power and influence of the country's rulers and their kingdoms."

ꕥ

V

The Maharajas of the Vijayanagara Empire: Karnataka

The Maharajas of the Vijayanagara Empire: Karnataka were a powerful and influential dynasty that ruled over the region of Karnataka in India for centuries. They were renowned for their grandeur and opulence, and their legacy is still felt in the region today.

The Vijayanagara Empire was founded in 1336 by two brothers, Harihara and Bukka Raya, who were both members of the Sangama dynasty. The brothers were able to unite the various warring factions in the region and create a powerful kingdom. The Vijayanagara Empire was one of the most powerful and prosperous empires in India during its time, and it was known for its grand architecture, art, and culture.

The Maharajas of the Vijayanagara Empire: Karnataka were renowned for their wealth and power. They were known for their lavish lifestyles and their patronage of the arts. They built grand palaces and temples, and they were also known for their patronage of literature and the sciences.

The Maharajas of the Vijayanagara Empire: Karnataka were also known for their military prowess. They were able to expand their kingdom and protect it from foreign invasions. They were also able to maintain a strong and stable government, which allowed them to maintain their power and influence in the region.

The Maharajas of the Vijayanagara Empire: Karnataka were also known for their religious tolerance. They allowed people of all faiths to practice their religion freely, and they were also known for their patronage of Hinduism, Buddhism, and Jainism.

The legacy of the Maharajas of the Vijayanagara Empire: Karnataka is still felt in the region today. Their grand palaces and temples are still standing, and their patronage of the arts and sciences is still remembered. Their religious tolerance and military prowess are also remembered, and their legacy is still felt in the region today. The Maharajas of the Vijayanagara Empire: Karnataka have left a lasting impact on the culture and history of South India. Their support of multiple religions has contributed to the rich cultural diversity of the region, and their grand monuments serve as a testament to their patronage of the arts and sciences. The Vijayanagara Empire was known for its prosperity and cultural achievements, and its legacy continues to be celebrated in Karnataka.

"The Indian royalty is a window into the country's rich cultural heritage,"

ꟻ

VI

The Maharajas of the Nizams: Hyderabad

The Maharajas of the Nizams: Hyderabad were a powerful dynasty that ruled over the Deccan region of India for centuries. The Nizams were the hereditary rulers of the princely state of Hyderabad, which was one of the largest and wealthiest states in India during the British Raj. The Nizams were renowned for their patronage of the arts, their lavish lifestyles, and their patronage of education and culture.

The Nizams of Hyderabad were descended from the Qutb Shahi dynasty, which had ruled the Deccan region since the 16th century. The first Nizam, Asaf Jah I, was appointed by the Mughal emperor Aurangzeb in 1724. He established the Asaf Jahi dynasty, which would rule Hyderabad until 1948.

The Nizams of Hyderabad were known for their grandeur and opulence. They built magnificent palaces, such as the Chowmahalla Palace, and constructed grand monuments, such as the Charminar. They also patronized the arts, commissioning works of art and literature, and sponsoring festivals and performances.

The Nizams were also renowned for their patronage of education and culture. They established several universities, such as the Osmania University, and supported the development of the Urdu language. They also established a number of libraries and museums, such as the Salar Jung Museum.

The Nizams of Hyderabad were also known for their philanthropy. They established hospitals, schools, and charitable trusts, and provided financial assistance to the poor. They also provided scholarships to students and supported the development of the arts.

The Nizams of Hyderabad were a powerful dynasty that left an indelible mark on the history and culture of India. Their patronage of the arts, their lavish lifestyles, and their philanthropy have left a lasting legacy. Their rule was a golden age for the Deccan region, and their influence is still felt in the architecture, literature, and music of the region. The Nizams‘ patronage of education has contributed to the growth of institutions of learning, such as the Osmania University, and their philanthropy has helped to improve the lives of many people in the region.

The Nizams’ legacy continues to be celebrated in Hyderabad, where their monuments, palaces, and other cultural institutions are considered major tourist attractions. Their grandeur and opulence have become an integral part of Hyderabad's cultural heritage, and their philanthropy is still remembered as an example of compassion and generosity. The Nizams' rule was a defining period in the history of India, and their legacy continues to inspire future generations.

"It is a reminder of the importance of preserving and celebrating India's unique history and traditions."

ꕤ

VII

The conservation and preservation of Indian Royal Heritage

The conservation and preservation of Indian royal heritage is an important part of understanding the cultural and historical significance of India's Maharajas and their kingdoms. For centuries, these royal families have been the custodians of India's rich cultural heritage, and their legacy has been passed down through generations.

The conservation and preservation of Indian royal heritage is a complex process that requires a multi-faceted approach. It involves the protection of monuments, artifacts, and other cultural artifacts, as well as the preservation of traditional customs and practices. In addition, it also involves the promotion of education and awareness about the importance of preserving India's royal heritage.

The conservation and preservation of Indian royal heritage is a challenging task, as it requires the cooperation of multiple stakeholders, including the government, local communities, and private organizations. The government has a key role to play in this process, as it is responsible for the protection of monuments and artifacts, as well as the promotion of education and awareness about the importance of preserving India's royal heritage.

Local communities also play an important role in the conservation and preservation of Indian royal heritage. They are responsible for the maintenance of monuments and artifacts, as well as the promotion of traditional customs and practices. Private organizations, such as museums and heritage societies, are also involved in the conservation and preservation of Indian royal heritage. They are responsible for the preservation of artifacts and monuments, as well as the promotion of education and awareness about the importance of preserving India's royal heritage.

The conservation and preservation of Indian royal heritage is a complex process that requires the cooperation of multiple stakeholders. It is essential to ensure that the preservation of India's royal heritage is done in a way that is respectful of the culture and traditions of the people. This is why it is important to involve local communities in the process, as they are the custodians of India's rich cultural heritage.

The conservation and preservation of Indian royal heritage is an important part of understanding the cultural and artifacts, future generations can learn about the rich history, traditions, and cultural achievements of these dynasties. In addition, it helps to boost tourism, which can provide economic benefits to local communities.

However, preserving India's royal heritage also requires significant financial resources and expertise. The government, as well as private organizations, play an important role in supporting the preservation of these monuments and artifacts. It is also important to ensure that the preservation process is carried out in a sustainable manner, taking into consideration the impact on the environment and local communities.

The conservation and preservation of India's royal heritage is a complex process that requires cooperation and collaboration among multiple stakeholders. By working together, it is possible to preserve these cultural treasures for future generations to appreciate and learn from.

"The Indian royalty is a symbol of the country's resilience and strength,"

ꕥ

VIII

The Maharajas of the British Raj: Princely States

The Maharajas of the British Raj were the rulers of the princely states of India during the period of British rule. These rulers were the most powerful and influential figures in the country, and their kingdoms were the most prosperous and influential in the region. The Maharajas of the British Raj were the epitome of power and wealth, and their influence extended far beyond their own borders.

The Maharajas of the British Raj were the descendants of the ancient Indian dynasties, and their rule was based on a system of patronage and loyalty. They were the custodians of the culture and traditions of India, and their rule was based on a system of justice and fairness. The Maharajas of the British Raj were the most powerful and influential figures in the country, and their kingdoms were the most prosperous and influential in the region.

The Maharajas of the British Raj were the most powerful and influential figures in the country, and their kingdoms were the most prosperous and influential in the region. They were the custodians of the culture and traditions of India, and their rule was based on a system of justice and fairness. The Maharajas of the British Raj were the epitome of power and wealth, and their influence extended far beyond their own borders.

The Maharajas of the British Raj were the most powerful and influential figures in the country, and their kingdoms were the most prosperous and influential in the region. They were the custodians of the culture and traditions of India, and their rule was based on a system of justice and fairness. The Maharajas of the British Raj were the epitome of power and wealth, and their influence extended far beyond their own borders.

The Maharajas of the British Raj were the most powerful and influential figures in the country, and their kingdoms were the most prosperous and influential in the region. They were the custodians of the culture and traditions of India, and their rule was based on a system of justice and fairness. The Maharajas of the British Raj were also known for their patronage of the arts and sciences, and their courts were renowned for their grandeur and opulence. They supported the development of institutions of learning, such as universities, and provided scholarships to students.

The legacy of the Maharajas of the British Raj is still felt today. Their grand palaces, monuments, and other cultural institutions are considered major tourist attractions, and their influence on the architecture, literature, and music of India is still evident. Their legacy of religious tolerance, justice, and fairness continues to inspire future generations, and their patronage of the arts and sciences has contributed to the growth and development of Indian culture.

However, the rule of the British Raj also had its drawbacks, as the British colonial government imposed many policies that marginalized and oppressed certain sections of society. Despite these challenges, the legacy of the Maharajas of the British Raj remains a major part of India's cultural heritage, and their influence is still celebrated and revered in the region.

"It is a reminder of the courage and determination of the people who have fought to protect their culture and traditions."

ꕤ

IX

The Maharajas and their Courts: Art, Architecture, and Culture

The Maharajas and their courts were renowned for their art, architecture, and culture. For centuries, the Indian Royalty has been a source of fascination and admiration for many. From the grandeur of their palaces to the intricate details of their clothing, the Maharajas and their courts have left an indelible mark on Indian culture.

The art of the Maharajas and their courts was a reflection of their wealth and power. From the grandeur of their palaces to the intricate details of their clothing, the Maharajas and their courts were renowned for their opulence and extravagance. The palaces of the Maharajas were adorned with intricate carvings, paintings, and sculptures, while their clothing was often made of the finest fabrics and adorned with precious jewels.

The architecture of the Maharajas and their courts was also a reflection of their wealth and power. The palaces of the Maharajas were often grand and elaborate, with intricate designs and lavish decorations. The architecture of the Maharajas and their courts was also a reflection of their culture and beliefs. Many of the palaces were built with Hindu and Islamic influences, and the architecture often featured elements of both religions.

The culture of the Maharajas and their courts was also a reflection of their wealth and power. The courts of the Maharajas were often filled with music, dance, and art. The courts were also a place of learning, with the Maharajas often hosting scholars and artists from around the world. The culture of the Maharajas and their courts was also a reflection of their beliefs and values, with many of the customs and traditions of the Maharajas and their courts still being practiced today.

The Maharajas and their courts have left an indelible mark on Indian culture. From the grandeur of their palaces to the intricate details of their clothing, the Maharajas and their courts have left a lasting legacy that continues to influence and shape Indian culture. Their patronage of the arts, literature, and sciences, as well as their religious tolerance, has had a lasting impact on the region and continues to inspire future generations. The Maharajas and their courts were also an important part of India's history, and their contributions to the country's rich cultural heritage are still recognized and celebrated today.

"The Indian royalty is a reminder of the beauty and grandeur of India's past," said a fourth.

ꕤ

X

The Maharajas and their Social and Political Roles

The Maharajas of India have long been revered for their immense wealth, power, and influence. Throughout history, they have played a significant role in the social, political, and cultural development of the country.

The Maharajas were the rulers of the various princely states of India, and their power and influence extended far beyond their own domains. They were the most powerful and influential figures in the country, and their decisions had a profound impact on the lives of their subjects.

The Maharajas were not only powerful rulers, but also patrons of the arts and culture. They were responsible for the development of many of India's most iconic monuments, such as the Taj Mahal and the Red Fort. They also supported the growth of literature, music, and the performing arts.

The Maharajas were also influential in the political arena. They were instrumental in the formation of the Indian National Congress, which was the first major political party in India. They also played a major role in the negotiations that led to the independence of India from British rule.

The Maharajas were also important figures in the social and religious life of India. They were patrons of Hinduism, Buddhism, and Jainism, and they supported the growth of these religions in their domains. They also supported the growth of education and healthcare in their domains, and they were responsible for the construction of many temples and other religious sites.

The Maharajas were also important figures in the economic life of India. They were responsible for the development of many industries, such as textiles, mining, and agriculture. They also supported the growth of trade and commerce in their domains.

The Maharajas were a powerful and influential force in India for centuries, and their legacy continues to this day. Their contributions to the social, political, and cultural development of India are undeniable, and their impact on the country is still felt today. This chapter of The Indian history is an important one, and the study of the Maharajas and their rule is essential to understanding the rich cultural heritage of India and its evolution over time. Their influence on India's economy, art, literature, and politics has left a lasting impact, and they will always be remembered as one of the defining features of India's rich history and cultural identity.

"It is a reminder of the importance of preserving and celebrating India's unique culture and traditions."

ஐ

XI

The Maharajas and their relationship with the British Raj

The Maharajas of India have a long and complex relationship with the British Raj. For centuries, the Maharajas were the rulers of their own kingdoms, with their own laws and customs. They were powerful and influential figures in India, and their relationship with the British Raj was often strained.

The British Raj was established in India in 1858, and the Maharajas were forced to accept British rule. Initially, the Maharajas were allowed to keep their titles and some of their power, but the British Raj gradually took control of more and more of their authority. The Maharajas were forced to accept British laws and regulations, and their power was slowly eroded.

The Maharajas were not always willing to accept British rule, and there were several instances of resistance. In some cases, the Maharajas were able to negotiate with the British Raj and retain some of their power. In other cases, the Maharajas were forced to accept British rule and were stripped of their titles and power.

The relationship between the Maharajas and the British Raj was complex and often strained. The Maharajas were powerful figures in India, and their relationship with the British Raj was often a source of tension. Despite the tensions, the Maharajas and the British Raj were able to come to an understanding and work together to maintain peace and stability in India.

The Maharajas and the British Raj had a long and complicated relationship, and it is an important part of India's history. The Maharajas were powerful figures in India, and their relationship with the British Raj was often strained.

Despite the tensions, the Maharajas and the British Raj were able to come to an understanding and work together to maintain peace and stability in India. This relationship is an important part of India's history, and it is essential to understand the complexities of the Maharajas and their relationship with the British Raj in order to gain a better understanding of India's past and present. The British Raj saw the Maharajas as valuable allies in their rule over India, and the Maharajas saw the British as a source of stability and security.

However, this relationship was not without its challenges,

as both sides had different interests and goals. The legacy of this relationship is still felt today, and it is important to study it in order to understand the complexities of India's past and its impact on its present.

"The Maharajas of India personified the grandeur and magnificence of a bygone era, and their legacy continues to inspire and captivate people to this day."

ꟷ

XII

The Maharajas and their Legacy in Modern India

The Maharajas of India have left an indelible mark on the country's culture and history. From the grandeur of their palaces to the intricate details of their clothing, the Maharajas have been a source of fascination for centuries.

The Maharajas were the rulers of India's princely states, which were semi-autonomous regions that were ruled by a local ruler. These rulers were often members of the royal family, and they had a great deal of power and influence over their subjects. The Maharajas were known for their lavish lifestyles, and they often had large palaces and extravagant clothing.

The Maharajas were also known for their patronage of the arts. They were patrons of music, dance, and literature, and they often commissioned works of art and architecture. The Maharajas were also known for their patronage of education, and they often established schools and universities.

The legacy of the Maharajas is still evident in modern India. Many of the princely states still exist, and the Maharajas' palaces and other monuments are still standing. The Maharajas' patronage of the arts is still evident in the country's vibrant cultural scene. The Maharajas' patronage of education is also still evident in the country's universities and schools.

The Maharajas and their legacy have had a profound impact on India's culture and history. From their patronage of the arts to their patronage of education, the Maharajas have left an indelible mark on the country. Their legacy is still evident in modern India, and their influence can still be seen in the country's vibrant cultural scene. The Maharajas and their legacy are an important part of India's history, and they deserve to be remembered and celebrated.

"The Indian Royalty was a symbol of power, wealth and influence, but they were also patrons of the arts and patrons of knowledge, leaving behind a rich cultural legacy."

ꙮ

XIII

The Maharaja Palaces and Forts as Tourist Attraction

India's Maharajas and their kingdoms have long been a source of fascination for travelers and historians alike. From the grandeur of the palaces and forts to the intricate details of the culture and history, the Indian Royalty has captivated the world for centuries.

The Maharaja Palaces and Forts are some of the most impressive and awe-inspiring tourist attractions in India. These majestic structures are a testament to the grandeur and power of the Maharajas and their kingdoms. From the majestic Amber Fort in Jaipur to the imposing Mehrangarh Fort in Jodhpur, these palaces and forts are a reminder of the grandeur of the Indian Royalty.

The palaces and forts of the Maharajas are a living testament to the culture and history of India. From the intricate carvings and artwork to the grand courtyards and gardens, these structures are a reminder of the grandeur of the Indian Royalty. Visitors can explore the grandeur of the palaces and forts, and learn about the culture and history of the Maharajas and their kingdoms.

The palaces and forts of the Maharajas are also a great way to experience the culture and history of India. Visitors can explore the grand courtyards and gardens, and learn about the customs and traditions of the Maharajas and their kingdoms. From the grandeur of the palaces and forts to the intricate details of the culture and history, visitors can gain a unique insight into the Indian Royalty.

The Maharaja Palaces and Forts are a must-see for any traveler to India. From the grandeur of the palaces and forts to the intricate details of the culture and history, these majestic structures are a reminder of the grandeur and power of the Maharajas and their kingdoms. Visitors can explore the grandeur of the palaces and forts, and learn about the rich cultural heritage of India. These palaces and forts are not just tourist attractions, but they are also an important part of India's cultural heritage and a testament to the rich history and traditions of the country. They are an integral part of India's cultural identity and a symbol of its rich heritage, making them a valuable and inspiring part of India's cultural and historical legacy.

"The Maharajas of India not only ruled with an iron fist, but they also had a heart of gold, providing for their people and contributing to the development of their regions."

ℵ

XIV

The Modern Indian Royalty and their Role in Society

The modern Indian royalty, despite the loss of political power, continues to play an important role in the social, cultural, and economic development of the country. The modern Indian royalty consists of the descendants of the former ruling families, who have managed to maintain their legacy and status in society despite the change in times. The modern Indian royalty is seen as a symbol of tradition, culture, and heritage, and they continue to play an important role in shaping the cultural identity of India.

The modern Indian royalty is often involved in a number of philanthropic and social initiatives aimed at promoting the welfare of their communities and improving the quality of life for the people. They are also involved in preserving the cultural heritage of their regions, and many of them have established museums, cultural centers, and heritage sites to showcase the rich cultural traditions of India.

The modern Indian royalty is also involved in the economic development of their regions, and many of them have established businesses and industries aimed at promoting economic growth and creating jobs for the people. They are also involved in the tourism industry, and many of them have opened up their palaces and forts to visitors, providing a unique insight into the rich cultural and historical heritage of India.

The modern Indian royalty is also involved in promoting education and providing opportunities for the people. Many of them have established schools and colleges, and they provide scholarships and financial assistance to students from underprivileged backgrounds. They are also involved in promoting sports and cultural activities, and they provide support to young athletes and artists.

The modern Indian royalty has a strong cultural and historical connection with the people, and they continue to play an important role in the social, cultural, and economic development of the country. Despite the loss of political power, the modern Indian royalty continues to maintain its influence and importance in the cultural landscape of India, and they are seen as a symbol of the rich cultural heritage and traditions of the country.

The modern Indian royalty continues to play an important role in the social, cultural, and economic development of the country. They are seen as a symbol of tradition, culture, and heritage, and they continue to play an important role in preserving the cultural heritage of India. Despite the loss of political power, the modern Indian royalty remains a powerful force in the cultural landscape of India, and their contributions to the country will continue to be remembered for generations to come.

"The Indian Royalty was a symbol of unity, diversity and strength, with each ruler leaving behind a unique legacy of their own that shaped the cultural and historical landscape of India."

ꕥ

XV

Conclusion: The ongoing significance of the Indian Royalty

The Indian Royalty has been a source of fascination for centuries, and its influence on Indian culture and history is undeniable. From the grandeur of the maharajas' palaces to the intricate details of their clothing and jewelry, the Indian Royalty has left an indelible mark on the country's culture. Even today, the legacy of the Indian Royalty is still evident in the form of monuments, festivals, and other cultural events.

The Indian Royalty has been a source of inspiration for many, and its influence can be seen in the works of writers, artists, and musicians. The maharajas' palaces and forts have been the subject of many books, films, and television shows. The maharajas‘ clothing and jewelry have been replicated in fashion shows and jewelry stores. The maharajas’ festivals and ceremonies have been celebrated in cities and villages across India.

The Indian Royalty has also been a source of pride for many Indians. The maharajas were seen as symbols of power and wealth, and their influence was felt throughout the country. The maharajas‘ palaces and forts were seen as symbols of strength and stability, and their festivals and ceremonies were seen as a way to celebrate the country’s culture and history.

The Indian Royalty has also been a source of controversy. The maharajas’ wealth and power have been seen as a source of inequality and oppression. The maharajas‘ palaces and forts have been seen as symbols of extravagance and excess. The maharajas’ festivals and ceremonies have been seen as a way to promote superstition and religious intolerance.

Despite the controversy, the Indian Royalty continues to be a significant part of Indian society and culture. In modern times, many former maharajas have taken on philanthropic and social causes, using their wealth and influence to support education, healthcare, and other initiatives aimed at improving the lives of people in their communities. Some have even entered into politics, using their position to bring about positive change in their regions.

In recent years, the Indian government has also recognized the importance of preserving the heritage and culture of the Indian Royalty. The government has taken steps to protect the palaces and forts of the maharajas, preserving them as important cultural and historical landmarks. The government has also established museums and cultural centers to promote and educate the public about the rich cultural heritage of the maharajas.

Despite their troubled past, the Indian Royalty continues to play an important role in modern-day India. Whether through their philanthropy, social activism, or cultural preservation, the maharajas continue to be a significant part of the fabric of Indian society. Today, the Indian Royalty is viewed as a reminder of the rich cultural heritage of India and the unique role that the maharajas played in shaping the country's history and future.

"The legacy of the Maharajas of India is not just limited to their wealth and grandeur, but also to the impact they had on their people, their region and the country as a whole, serving as a reminder of the rich cultural heritage of India."

ꕥ

Other Books Of The Author

1. The Moments When I Met God
2. Kashiyile Theertha Pathangal
3. GURU GYAN VANI
4. Abhiprerak Gita
5. ASSI SE JAIN GHAT TAK
6. Hopelessness of Arjuna
7. The Soul and It's True Nature
8. Sense of Action (Karma)
9. Action through Wisdom
10. Action through Wisdom
11. THEORY AND PRACTICAL OF EVERY ACTION
12. LOGICAL UNDERSTANDING OF THE SUPREME
13. THE IMPERISHABLE SUPREME
14. Yatra Nishadraj se Hanuman Ghat Tak
15. Yatra Karnatak Ghat se Raja Ghat Tak
16. Yatra Pandey Ghat se Prayagraj Ghat Tak
17. Yatra Ranjendra Prasad Ghat se Dattatreya Ghat Tak
18. YaatraSindhiya Ghat se Gwaliar Ghat Tak
19. Yatra Mangala Gauri Ghat se Hanuman Gadhi Ghat Tak
20. Yatra Gaay Ghat Se Nishad Ghat Tak
21. MAA GANGA, GHATEN EVM UTSAV
22. Ganga Arti Dev Deepavali evam Any Utsav
23. Potentials of Digitalized India
24. VEDIC CONSCIOUSNESS
25. A Brief Introduction to Vedic Science
26. Kashi ke Barah Jyotirling
27. IMPACT OF MOTIVATION
28. Let's have a Milky Way Journey
29. Color Therapy in a Nutshell

30. Rigveda in a Nutshell
31. Yajurveda in a Nutshell
32. Samveda in a Nutshell
33. Atharva Veda in a Nutshell
34. Ayushman Bhava - Ayurveda
35. Srimad Bhagavad Gita and Upanishad Connection
36. Srimad Bhagavad Gita - an attempt to summarize each chapter.
37. Facts and Impact of Nakshatra
38. Astro Gems - NAVARATNA
39. Ekadashi - A Concise Overview
40. A Concise View of Hanuman Chalisa
41. Inspirational Gita
42. Nakshatraranyam
43. Summary of 18 Mahapuranas
44. Synopsis of 18 Upa Puranas
45. Rigvediya Upanishads
46. Shukla Yajurvediya Upanishads
47. Krishna Yajurvediya Upanishads
48. Samavediya Upanishads
49. Atharvavediya Upanishads
50. The Seven Great Sages
51. From Rocket Scientist to President Dr. APJ Abdul Kalam
52. The Visionary's Voice - Quotes of Dr. APJ Abdul Kalam
53. The Wisdom of Swami Vivekananda: Insights and Inspiration from a Legendary Spiritual Teacher
54. Ayurvedic Remedies from the Garden
55. Sages and Seers
56. Rising Strong – Motivational Stories of Women
57. Beyond Flames -Mystery stories of Funeral Ghat Manikarnika
58. The Origins of Tulsi: A Look at the Mythological Roots of the Plant"

59. The Holistic Cow: A Look at the Physical, Spiritual, and Cultural Importance of Cows in India
60. Arts of Healing
61. Exploring the Divine
62. Understanding Five Elements
63. The Etymology of Ram
64. Symbols of India
65. Voice of Change (About Speeches of Great Men)
66. She Speaks (About Speeches of Great Women)
67. Patriotism on Celluloid – Brief About Patriotic Films
68. The Music of Motivation: A Brief Guide to Inspirational Film Songs
69. **Unlocking the Secrets of the Dashopanishads**
70. A Cultural Mosaic
71. Ancient Traditions, Modern Minds
72. Ecos of Ancient Wisdom
73. Beneath the Surface
74. From Temples to Ashrams
75. Sages of the Subcontinent
76. The Art of Healling (Ayurveda, Yoga & Naturopathy)
77. Indian Kitchen
78. The Festivals of India
79. The Indian Epics Retold
80. The Power of Mantras
81. The Indian River Ganges
82. The Indian Architecture
83. Rites of Passage
84. The Indian Silk Road
85. The Indian Literature
86. The Indian Villages
87. The Indian Folks & Crafts
88. The Way of Buddha
89. The Ramayan of Tulsidas

90. Astrological Remedies
91. The Secret Power of Motivation
92. Secret of Developing your Inner Strength
93. The Secret Path to Motivation
94. The Art and Secret of Positive Thinking
95. The Secrets of Practicing Ethical Living
96. Indian Art and Painting
97. The Indian Herbalism
98. Bharatanatyam to Kathak
99. Exploring India's Astrological Remedies
100. The Indian Festival of Flowers
101. Indian Handicrafts
102. The Splashes of Joy – India's Colour Festival
103. The Indian Science of Astrology
104. The Indian Mythology
105. Path to Enlightenment
106. The Indian Spirituality for Children
107. Aromas of India
108. The Secrets of Healthy Relationships
109. Ancestral Ties
110. The Indian Street Food
111. Discovering America
112. The Indian Textile
113. Listening to Motivational Speeches
114. Taste of India
115. A Cultural Journey through Indian Nuptials
116. Motivational Quote for Change
117. Secret Strategies for Making Money
118. Secrets to Cultivate a Positive Mindset
119. A Tapestry of Cultures: Exploring India from Kashmir to Kanyakumari
120. Achieving Your Dreams with Resilience: Secret Strategies for Overcoming Obstacles

121. Innovative Startups - 25 Startup Ideas to Spark Your Business Creativity
122. Export Management: Strategies for Global Success
123. Exporting from India - A Step by Step Guide
124. Finance Fundamentals: Mastering Financial Management for Business Success
125. Global Growth Strategies for International Business Development
126. Marketing Mastery: Unlocking the Secrets of Modern Marketing
127. Operations Mastery: Managing the Flow of Value in Business
128. Strategic Business Management: Navigating the Modern Business Landscape
129. Human Resource Management Strategies for Building and Managing a High Performance Team
130. The Indian Landscapes and Nature: An Exploration Of India's Natural Beauty And Diversity
131. The Indian Street Performances: A Cultural Exploration of India's Street Performances
132. Affirming Your Self-Worth: Strategies for Achieving Emotional Wellbeing
133. Cultivating Self-Discipline: Secrets Methods for Achieving Your Goals
134. Embracing Change: Strategies for Adapting to Life's Challenges
135. Embracing Your Uniqueness: Secret Strategies for Living an Authentic Life
136. Finding Motivation in Despondency: Coping with Difficult Times
137. Embracing Change
138. Learning to Love Yourself
139. Managing Time for Yourself

140. Unlock the keys to Self-Motivation
141. Secret to Boost Confidence
142. Unlocking your Potential: A Path to Inner-strength & Success
143. Secrets to Develop Authentic Relationship
144. Secrets to Build a Successful Career
145. Secrets to Live with Gratitude
146. Secrets to Create a Life of Abundance
147. Secrets to Cultivate Self-Awareness
148. The Power of Helping Hands
149. Finding Your Passion
150. The Indian Mythical Creatures
151. The Indian Women Saints
152. The Wisdom of the Saints
153. "The Indian Royalty: A Cultural and Historical Exploration of India's Maharajas and their kingdom"
154. The Mystic Land: A Cultural and Spiritual Exploration of India"

Contact

DR. JAGADEESH PILLAI

MBA & PhD in Vedic Science

Four Times Guinness World Record Holder

Winner of Mahatma Gandhi Vishwa Shanti Puraskar and Global Peace Ambassador

Gemology, Astro & Vastu Consultant - Spiritual Counselor

Consultant for designing World Record Ideas

Efficient Tarot Card Reader

9839093003

myrichindia@gmail.com

drjagadeeshpillai@facebook

drjagadeeshpillai@instagram
jagadeeshpillai@youtube

www. JAGADEESHPILLAI.com

|| LOKAHA SAMASTHAHA SUKHINO BHAVANTU ||

ഇ

Printed by Libri Plureos GmbH in Hamburg,
Germany